Last of the Big Three Caddies

Last of the Big Three Caddies

Stories of Hall of Fame Caddie Alfred "Rabbit" Dyer

John Downing

Clearview Press, Inc
Palm Coast, Florida

Last of the Big Three Caddies
Stories of Hall of Fame Caddie Alfred "Rabbit" Dyer

Front Cover Photo:
PCA MEDIA HALL OF FAME LIBRARY USED BY PERMISSION

Back Cover Photo:
BLACK KNIGHT INTERNATIONAL ARCHIVES USED BY PERMISSION

Photography throughout the book (as noted) by:
PPS. 18, 21, 22, 25, 27, 28, 52, 97, 120, 122-126, 127, 128, 129, 131
JOHN DOWNING

PPS. 54, 58, 62, 64, 67, 82, 84
BLACK KNIGHT INTERNATIONAL ARCHIVES USED BY PERMISSION

P.74 AP WIRE PHOTO VIA WIRE FROM LONDON, NEWSPAPER ARCHIVES
P.78 AP PHOTO

PPS. 90, 91, 92, 93, 96, 104
ALFRED DYER

P. 107 CADDYBYTES.COM

Articles courtesy of AP wire service via Newspaper Archives
PPS. 29, 59-60, 72-73

Editing by Tom Wallace
Book cover and interior design & layout by Kathleen M. Shea

ISBN: 978-1-935795-17-9 (soft cover)
LCCN: 2013944921

ClearView Press, Inc.
Post Office Box 353431
Palm Coast, FL 32135-3431

Printed in the United States of America

Acknowledgements

I would like to say thank you to all of the people who believed in me to make this book happen. Heather gave me her full support and helped me deal with a few of the people who were nonbelievers. A special thanks also to Kary and Jeff Adams, photographers and rock stars, who Rabbit just adores and who keep his spirits up. What happy people they are, and a blessing in my life.

Special thanks to Margarita Pas with the law firm Samuel Oliver in Darien, Georgia, Rich Styles radio host at www.back9boys.com, and Steve French for pre-ordering to help us out.

Foreword

South Africa with Jim and Carol Thorpe

"It was a damp grey day back in 1979. We lived in Buffalo, NY, so I suppose the weather was seasonal. The PGA tour season had concluded for the year and we were looking to the sky for funds to sustain us until the 1980 season began. The telephone rang out of the clear blue, and at the other end was Alfred "Rabbit" Dyer. Rabbit had gone on a mission to find us. He must have put in some work on that one, because not many people knew I had taken a position with the New York State Legislator. I don't remember exactly how Rabbit got a working telephone number for us, but I am so happy he found us. We owe our South African experience to our dear friend's diligence.

We had plenty to do before we departed. There was a two-year-old to get care for, and we had to get out shots and passports, and make travel arrangements. Check, check, check. After the excitement wore off, the big question came into play—do we break the unwritten sports boycott? Hell yeah, because I want to see what's going on in this country. We might be able to tell a story that could help someone. I told plenty of stories hoping they got to the right ears.

Travel to South Africa required visas so we went to the SA Embassy in NY, mentioned Gary Player's name, and we were out in ten minutes. The flight was absolutely grueling. It was eighteen hours over water because South African Airway was forbidden to fly in African air space. Jim needs his comfort zone and got so antsy on the plane that I had to piss him off just to give him something to think about besides the flight.

Finally we landed in Johannesburg. We deplaned, claimed our bags, and proceeded to customs. Our bags were searched, and then the question that I was not ready for came. "Do you have any books?" I did have a paperback novel and told them so. The customs officer looked like he was straight out of Nazi Germany. Jim gave me that look that said, what have you done? I was questioned about the book's contents. It was taken, inspected, and returned. I did not ask any questions.

By the time we got through with that, all we wanted to see was a man with a sign that had our name on it. What a vision he was, standing there waiting to escort us to our mini-van. On the way out of the airport we ran into Calvin Peete and his wife headed back to the USA. Calvin had been invited to the first series of tournament. We kind of wanted him to give us a feel for what was in store for us. He just said it was different, but we would enjoy ourselves. With that, he and his wife dashed off to their flight. I remember it being a good clip from the airport to the hotel. As much as I wanted to, I couldn't stay awake. When I came to, we were at the hotel in downtown Johannesburg.

We got checked into our room, and the phone rang. Jim and I looked at one another wondering who could know we were there. I hadn't even had a chance to call home to let my family have the emergency contact number.

I picked up the phone, and, yes you guessed right, it was Rabbit. We were so happy to hear his voice because we felt like fish out of water. We had no idea where we were allowed to go or who we could talk to. Calvin had told us it would be different. Rabbit gave us a few minutes to freshen up, and he advised us that he was going to take us to see things we weren't supposed to see.

I don't know how he was able to find a car, but he got one. We all crammed ourselves into the little compact, and off we went. Surprisingly he navigated the streets like he lived there. Rabbit told us he had some friends he wanted us to meet. We ended up in a rundown housing project that was reserved for black people. When he knocked a voice responded in a thick local accent and asked us in.

The three of us entered, and a portly lady was sitting quietly at a table in a sparsely furnished cinder block unit. She appeared to have the weight of the world on her shoulders. The lady rose to give us all hugs. That hug seemed to convey such desperation that I wanted to put her in my bag and take her home with me. I remember how honored she said she felt that we had come to visit her and her family. Two of her young daughters burst into the apartment and exchanged words in Afrikaans. Sometimes the universal language called mother lets you know what's being said without understanding the words. And by the way the woman responded, we knew something was brewing. The girls stayed for a few minutes and dashed back out the door. Rabbit asked the mother what was going on with the girls and why they were not in school.

The girls had completed the eighth grade, so there was no more school for them, because they were black. For the same reason, jobs were not easy to find. Whites preferred the blacks for domestic jobs. This poor mother was anguishing day in and day out over what was going to become of her daughters. I do not know if there was a father in picture.

The slamming of the door woke the only son, who was sleeping in a room just behind a curtain. He emerged and was introduced by his mom. We could tell how proud she was of him by the way she talked about his budding boxing career. We gave him encouraging words about what the future held for him in boxing. I remember that the girls had voiced some discontent with their conditions in English, but their mother stopped them. She said you never knew who was listening. Rabbit concurred, and we left moments later. I remember her telling me to think of them when I got back home. I must say I have truly kept my promise to her because I have thought of her and her children often. I have prayed that they would experience some form of improvement in their station in life.

From there we drove down a highway that was bordered by

a chain link fence. One sharp turn and we were in Soweto, the community that was designated for the blacks. The roads were unpaved and rutted. There was so much smoke from cooking fires that you couldn't help but choke and cough. Happy children were everywhere—they ran, they jumped rope, they kicked soccer balls. The funniest thing we saw was two teenage girls pushing one another like a fight was about to erupt. But there was no fight. They began to dance in competition to cheering crowds of friends. Now that is the way to settle differences. Rabbit commented on how American kids should follow some of these examples. We had been warned not to go to Soweto, but Rabbit assured us we were back where it all started for us. We had flown eighteen hours and had no rest or food, but our curiosity just had the best of us. Our exploits lasted until dark. Rabbit dropped us off in front of the hotel. Jim, not being the adventurous type made it a point to invite Rabbit back the next day. We were given an agenda the tournament had set up for us.

We went to our room and tried to settle back into our jet lagged bodies. We were sent an invitation to lunch with the Player family at one of their many South African homes. We arrived and were greeted by Gary, Vivian, and their daughter Jenny. The house was amazing. It had a huge grass roof that Gary explained was a natural air conditioner. We got a quick tour, and the African ladies that worked for Gary were quite taken by Jim. Gary noticed and invited them in to meet us. Gary speaks about twelve African dialects. He translated for one woman who, in her language, asked to touch Jim's arms because they were so big. Naturally, Gary looked to me for the nod of approval. I figured, what the heck this must be an African custom, so I let her go for it. The look on Gary's face was priceless because that came straight from left field. Rabbit was pretty tickled and explained that the blacks in South Africa were really impressed by height and athletic bodies.

We got thru the touchy feely, and out came Gary's dogs. I swear they were so big you could have put a saddle on them and ridden them around the property. We were told we had nothing to fear as long as we didn't look threatening to the family. Okay. I just wanted to know where to stand. We spent a wonderful afternoon with Gary and his family before returning to our hotel.

Early on the third day, a van was sent for us to take us to Saba Game Reserve. Saba was about two hours from Johannesburg. We checked into our hut—yes a hut with grass roof and all and only one hour of electricity per day and no locks on the doors. We were taken on nature walks and rides in the middle of the night to watch lions make kills up close. The game reserve was managed by the whites and worked by women and men from a neighboring African tribe.

There was a small pool near our hut that Jim decided to cool off in at high noon one day, but when he looked in and saw the water snakes taking a swim he returned quickly. The men on the reserve did not work that much. It was the custom for them to watch the women work—literally. They sat under shade trees and watched the women work. If there were snakes to kill or something to hunt, the men would do that.

At night huge bonfires were light and dinner was served under a hundred-year-old eucalyptuses tree. The girls would do tribal dances to entertain us. The group that had come to the game reserve included Jim, myself, Arnold Palmer, Sandy Lye, Nancy Dyer, Jenny Player, Bo and Norman out of Atlanta, Georgia, and a few others with the tournament.

There were countless golf tales told and jokes that had our sides hurting. All in all Saba was a fun side trip. By the time we left Saba it had sunk in that we were in Africa, the place where it started for everyone, the birth place of all humanity. We saw animals walking around that were twice the size of anything you see in local zoos. I really looked at the faces of the people. They were beautiful faces, but they were sad faces. Apartheid was a crime against humanity.

The Africans were really uncomfortable doing the same things for Jim and me as they were doing for the whites. We spent three days on the reserve, and, believe me, that was plenty for a city girl like me.

We were off to the tournament, and our group was loaded onto several mini-vans with our luggage and taken to a private airstrip where three small planes were waiting. Two of the planes were for passengers, and one was for the luggage. They decided that everything would fit on two planes, so the other plane was sent back to the hanger. We took off down the runway and the pilot struggled to get the plane airborne because it was dangerously overloaded. The flight was uneventful until the young pilot decided to do what seemed like a nose dive into a river so his girlfriend could get a close-up view of the hippos that where feeding there. Arnold Palmer and Gary Player were on the other plane that came close enough to our plane to read the lips of their passengers. Arnold Palmer is a pilot and he knows the rules and regulations of air safety, he was extremely vexed at the pilots' conduct during the flight. He made it painfully clear that he was going to file a formal complaint against both of the pilots. When he calmed down he got that uh-huh look on his face.

He turned to Gary and said, "The headline would have read Gary Player and Arnold Palmer Lost in Airplane Crash, not Arnold Palmer and Gary Player Lost in Airplane Crash."

Gary scratched his head and said, "Yes, laddy, there would have been plenty of widows and orphans."

We later found out that we were separated from death by no more than eighteen inches. The planes were so close over the river it is a miracle there was not a midair collision. With that said, God had a journey for each person in our group.

We arrived in Sun City, a brand new resort and casino that was cut out of the South African bush. We got checked into the hotel and ready for the first round of the tournament.

A few days later Rabbit found us again. This time he came with a black man that worked as a gold courier. We had been told about the diamond district and shopping areas. Our plane did not leave until that evening. Rabbit's friend arranged a tour of the distributor, and transportation to the department stores. When we were dropped off in downtown Johannesburg, there was a sea of humanity. Everything there was at a premium. You could tell in the people's faces that this country was ready to explode. I did not want to be there when it happened, because they knew we were not from there.

After buying a cute little trinket for our daughter as we promised, we headed back to the hotel and looked out of the window until it was time for our airport pick up. Rabbit came back alone this time. He spoke about how it saddened him to see our people treated under the apartheid system. I had to remind him that our country had its own form of racial discrimination, and he concurred. At that time the South African government was run solely by whites, and it remained that way until 1991. Rabbit was passionate about not allowing himself to be treated like the oppressed masses in South Africa. He was a bit of a local celebrity, and being Gary Player's guest/employee made life extremely good while he was visiting and working there.

We are very happy to have known Rabbit and to be able to contribute to this book. We wish him all the best."

Jim and Carol Thorpe

Dedications

This book is dedicated to all of the caddies I shagged balls and caddied with. To all of the caddies who changed in the parking lots or the woods, and to all the caddies who have passed away from our era that worked so hard to get the game of golf to where it is today. To Mitch, Hobo, Puzzle, Killer, Jimmy Clark, Golfball, Angelo, Creamy, Faye and all the others from my time.

To my children.

Rabbit Dyer

This book is dedicated to my Dad, Joseph Ronald Downing, who taught me the game of golf and took me to tournaments as a kid to see the Big Three and many of the greatest golfers of all time, many of whom Rabbit caddied for. I was as much of a fan of their caddies as I was the players. To my little brother, Matt, who has become a good friend of, and believer in, my project. To my Mom, Bea, who always knew I could do it somehow and my daughters, Sonni and baby Kailani, Heather and her parents Woody and Diane.

John Downing

John and Rabbit 2012

Introduction

John Downing

Rabbit was introduced to me in June 2012 on a fishing dock in Hammock Beach, Florida where a guy was there pulling crab traps while Rabbit and I attempted to catch some fish.

Neither one of us do much fishing. We were really just enjoying the sunset, watching some dolphins play in the Intracoastal Waterway, and shooting the breeze. Eventually we realized we had much more in common than we imagined, and had crossed paths many years ago.

Subsequently we spent many days talking, and he told me stories from his life and his iconic career on the PGA Tour with golf's greatest. I asked him if I could write this book about, not only his accomplishments and wins, but how he got where he is now, what motivated him to be the man he is, and how he became so well respected in this small, elite class of athletes that have made history in the game of golf around the world.

He told me there were others who had interviewed him for articles and blogs and made him offers to write a book, but he was not comfortable with them and now it just felt right. I feel honored to be given this opportunity.

Rabbit agreed to let me tape record many hours of conversations with him and told me if I can get a book out of it, more power to me.

He's a very humble man, and doesn't like a lot of attention. He lives a quiet life in St. Augustine, Florida, and is enjoying his retirement by the ocean.

These days you may find him walking along St. George Street in Old Saint Augustine, or walking over the Bridge of Lions. He still believes a good five-mile walk is the key to health. From time to time he hangs out over at the Murray Brothers' Caddyshack Restaurant at the World Golf Village telling stories about the good old days with Ben Hogan, "Champagne" Tony Lema, Chi Chi Rodriguez, Lee Trevino, and, of course, Gary Player.

Rabbit still loves to caddie and tell his stories. He is often invited and is always available for corporate golf events, outings as a guest speaker, and "Caddie for a Day," where he will still caddie for you personally. Just recently as we are writing this book, Gary Player called Rabbit back into service to caddie for him at the Liberty Mutual Legends of Golf at the Club at Savannah Harbor and in Houston at the Insperity Open where the Big Three will be reuniting once again and maybe for the last time.

John Downing

John Downing

Rabbit and Gary Player 2013
Liberty Mutual Legends of Golf

John Downing

Gary Player, Jack Nicklaus and Rabbit
2013 Liberty Mutual Legends of Golf

Introduction

Alfred "Rabbit" Dyer

Many Firsts for the Record Books

The first British Open was played in 1860. It took over a hundred years for the first black caddie to carry a bag at that tournament. That was me, in 1974, when I was working for Gary Player. They say I am one of the original "big three caddies" with Angelo Argea (who worked for Jack Nicklaus for many years) and Creamy Caroline (Arnold Palmer's longtime caddie). They've left us, so I'm the last of the big three to tell the stories and continue the legacy, hence the name of my book The Last of the Big Three Caddies.

I have a lot of firsts. I was the first black caddie (we were called "colored" back then) to work at Arizona's Thunderbird Country Club, to caddie and win the British Open, and the first American black caddie to carry a bag in South Africa. I am the first black to caddie in all four Majors.

The first professional golfer I ever caddied for was Ben Hogan. I also caddied for Tony Lema in 1960 when he won his first tournament at the Hesperia Open, which was my first win. Dave Stockton won his first tournament 1967—The Colonial in Texas—with me carrying his bag, and I was on Dan Sikes bag in

1963 when he had his first win at Doral. Dan Sikes ("the golfing lawyer") was the University of Florida's first All-American golfer.

Gary Player had a lot of firsts too. He was the first foreigner to be number one on the money list on the US Tour, the first foreigner to win the Masters, and the first player to win the British Open in three separate decades. We had a lot of firsts between the two of us, and working with him is truly an experience I've cherished all of my life.

I told John as he was writing this book for me that back in the beginning we were called colored caddies, because that's how blacks were referred to in the times of segregation. The term colored has now evolved into black, and/or African American, and I personally don't care how I'm referred to, as long as it's respectfully. I've been through it all, not only here in the US, but in South Africa during apartheid, and in Europe. Just recently, the day before my 76th birthday, I was in a restaurant parking lot when a man in a pickup truck pulled in next to me and banged his door into the side of my car. He got out and started walking the other way. I said to him, "Aren't you going to at least apologize?" He turned around and called me a name I haven't heard in years, and I have rarely been called the N-word to my face. He didn't realize how big I was until I walked around to the other side of the car and it was one, two, bap, bap, and his lights were out! I may be 76, but I can still defend myself.

I am just a person like everyone else, and color never will affect my belief that a person is a person, and we all have to work hard to achieve our own dreams and goals. I have been called every name referring to the color of my skin—and in several languages. Color should not make any difference. So when you're striving to achieve your goals, the color of your skin should never matter, no matter who you are or what you do. I'm sure Gary Player will agree with me on that. Gary was a big influence on the PGA's black players and black caddies here in America, South Africa, and Europe. He was very instrumental and did everything he could to eradicate apartheid and discrimination, not just in South Africa but worldwide, and I'm proud to have been his partner for so long during those times.

John Downing

Lee Trevino, Jack Nicklaus, Gary Player and Rabbit
Liberty Mutual Legends of Golf Course 2013

I just heard on a radio show the other day that Tiger Woods was suppose to be the break-through black man to turn the corner on color and open the gates for black golfers of his time, but some complained that he hasn't met their expectations in the timeframe they expected—not enough black golfers have emerged yet. Why does this conversation need to be brought up so often still?

What about Charlie Sifford, Jim Thorpe, Lee Elder, Calvin Peete and Jim Dent who came way before Tiger? There were more black PGA players in 1976 and before than there are now on the Tour. I don't think it should be Tiger's responsibility to carry that on his shoulders. If you want something bad enough you have to go and earn it, no matter what color you are.

A caddie's job is not just to carry the bag. A caddie is the golfer's copilot. He has to be confident, learn the course, walk the yardage, and never look nervous. If the golfer sees that you're nervous, he could get nervous. There's no place for being nervous or scared on the golf course. I'm a friend, a consultant, and a psychologist. Rule number one: if I want to keep my job, I have to know when to speak and when to bite my tongue. If I'm asked for my opinion I will give it, but once the pro makes his decision it's his decision not mine. If it's the wrong decision we move on, and he takes responsibility and doesn't blame the caddie.

I believe the reasons I was able to stay with Gary Player for close to twenty years—and be requested over and over by the best players in the world and countless celebrities, presidents and CEO's—was for the fact that I got to know them on a level like no one else, and I cared. Not only did I know their swings, I knew their mood swings. If a player was having a bad day I could usually figure out why and help to get him back in focus or in line, and I could always make him laugh.

Walking the course and preparing yardages and pin placements for the pro was essential. It's much more than just getting yardages from sprinkler heads. I learned the distances to the foot and knew how far the golfer I was caddying for could hit each club. I would find landmarks—a tree, a bush, or the top or bottom of a bunker—and have measurements from there. I took the extra time to get to know these yardages from every angle and obstacle to prepare him for any challenging shots. And, as you know, there are always going to be those challenging shots.

My life is full of great stories, and my friend who helped me write this book says I'm the Forest Gump of golf. Gary Player calls me The Muhammad Ali of golf. As of now I haven't seen the movie Forest Gump, but I hope that by the time this book is published I will have seen it, and, who knows, maybe I'll caddie for Tom Hanks some day.

I guess I've had hardships like everyone else, but I've also had the opportunity to travel all over the country and the world and be a part of history both on and off the golf course. There are so many accomplishments I'm proud of, and some not so good experiences. But that's life. You take the good and the bad. You have to make the best and most of all of them. They asked Gary Player how much of his success was luck, and he told them the more he practices and plays, the luckier he gets. Luck is a direct result of practice. So here are some parts of my life you don't know. I hope you enjoy these stories.

John Downing

Rabbit and Gary Player
2013 Liberty Mutual Legends of Golf

Alfred "Rabbit" Dyer

John Downing

Christmas 2012 – Rabbit signing presents

AP Wire Service

Add 'Rabbit' To Grand Slam List

WASHINGTON (AP) - "Who's that with all those people around him, asking autographs?" somebody was heard to ask at the Congressional Club, site of the PGA Golf Championship. "Oh, that's Jack Nicklaus," a companion replied. "Not him—I know Jack Nicklaus. That other guy?" "Oh, you mean the tall guy with the wide-brimmed straw hat? Everybody knows him. That's 'Rabbit.' "

That was a true scene and a true comment. One of the most familiar and flamboyant figures at any gold tournament on this continent or overseas is a tall, stringbean black man named Alfred Dyer. Call him "Rabbit." "I am the only caddie in the world to carry clubs in the Grand Slam," Rabbit said. "When I caddied for Gary Player in the 1974 British Open I was the first black caddie in that tournament in 104 years." That in itself, is enough to make Rabbit a celebrity. No other bag carrier has plied his trade in the big four prestigious tournaments—the Masters, U.S. and British Opens and the PGA.

The reason is simple. The Masters uses only Augusta caddies. Until recent years, the other three events barred tour bag toters. So it took some fast shuffling to make the Grand Slam-even if the only one he won was the 1974 British Open with Player. "I caddied in the Masters from 1962 through 1971, off and on," Rabbit explained. "I hauled dubs for Tony Lema and Lionel Hebert, among others. I've been caddying for Player since 1962 when I got him in a blind draw in New Orleans.

Dyer grew up in New Orleans, since moving to East Orange, N.J. But don't ever try to catch him at home. Like Player, whose stage is the world, Rabbit is always on the road. He's a golf gypsy. Player is one of four who have won the four major championships. The others have been Gene Sarazen, Ben Hogan and Jack Nicklaus. It's an exclusive club.

CHAPTER 1

Innocent Adversity

My mother was a wonderful lady. She worked at the Zatarain's factory in New Orleans, and I can never forget the smell of all those onions and spices on her when she walked in the door. My sister, Lorraine was a big help raising me and our brothers. My Dad had left us with my Mom to raise when they split up.

When I was sixteen a terrible thing happened at home. There was an argument between my mother and our stepdad. As they were arguing, my brother and I saw him move toward her with a brick in his hand. I jumped in between them to stop him from hitting her. It was all happening very fast, and before I could stop him my older brother, much smaller than me, came at him from behind grabbed with a kitchen knife. Before I could do anything he had reached over my shoulder and stabbed him in the chest. My brother panicked and ran outside.

I pulled the knife out of my stepdad's chest to try to save him, but he died right there on the floor in front of me. Our neighbor lady heard the commotion and ran over, only to see me holding the knife with blood all over me and the floor. It was utter chaos, and my older brother was nowhere to be found.

In New Orleans back in those days you were presumed guilty on the spot, no questions asked especially if you were black. Even though my mom did her best to tell them I didn't do it, they wouldn't believe her, so I spent four months in a New Orleans jailhouse. Believe me you did not want to be a sixteen year old teenager in that jailhouse. I wasn't in a juvenile detention—I was in with adults. It was a blessing that I was bigger than most kids my age, and I knew how to fight, since I grew up with seven brothers. I volunteered for mop duty so I could keep that big stick next to me at all times, even when I slept. No one ever messed with me.

Four months later they found my brother on the run in Alabama where he turned himself in. Soon after being arrested he confessed, and they released me that same day.

A basketball scholarship I had worked so hard for was taken away because of that, and my dreams of being a professional athlete were shattered. And that's why I didn't go to college.

Several years later, after my brother was released from prison, he was at club Desire in the Ninth Ward where he got into a fight over a girl. He was stabbed in the neck and killed. They said he got the ultimate punishment, but we knew he was just defending my mother. My sister, Lorraine, is still living in New Orleans, my brothers, Bernard, Faye, and Melvin, are in New Orleans too. We've never spoken of the incident since then, and this is the first time I've told the story.

CHAPTER 2

Cross Country Calamities

April 4, 1968 I was caddying the Memphis Open on the Southern Swing Tour at the Colonial Country Club. This was a beautiful course. We always looked forward to being there, and the prize money was some of the best on the tour.

All of the traveling caddies always stayed at the Lorraine Hotel because it was considered the nicest hotel in town and many celebrities and musicians stayed there—Ray Charles, Wilson Picket, and Aretha Franklin just to name a few.

This particular time I believe I was in room 216. It was a Tuesday, and I was leaving early that morning for work, I had to walk the course and get the yardages to be prepared for the practice round.

Martin Luther King Jr. was standing on the balcony above me, talking with his entourage; they seemed happy and were very friendly to me. I had seen him there before, and we would always wave and say hello to each other. That same evening, when I came back from work about 7:00 p.m., there was yellow police tape wrapped around the building, and police cars were everywhere.

People were crying. They all looked they were in a state of shock. I went into the office to find out what had happened. They told me at the front desk told that Martin Luther King Jr. had just been shot that morning only a short time after I waved to him on that balcony.

From my room I could see the window across the street where the shot was fired from and the police tape all around that building too. It was a sad day for everyone.

The caddies I traveled with were the hardest working caddies on the tour, always looking out for each other. It was a brotherhood; I guess you could call us a band of caddies. When we had down time we didn't spend much of it resting. We played just as hard as we worked even if just one of us had money we shared what we had, we helped each other out and we always watched each other's backs. It was a necessity to survive on the road for so long, none of us had credit cards or bank accounts back then but we always had cash with us.

The tour took my brother Faye and me to Dallas, Texas, in 1963 where Julius Boros won the Colonial, with Palmer and Nicklaus right behind him. Julius was the first one to win more than once at Colonial in Texas, after Ben Hogan won consecutively in 1950, and 1951. Julius Boros won in 1952 and Hogan again in 1953.

Julius was best known for his flop shot (a short lob from the high grass close to the green), for his wins at the 1952 and 1963 US Open, and for placing fifth or better at the US Open six times.

Faye and I were staying together in a cheap boarding house next to the local bar where we could shoot pool at night after a long day on the course. Both Faye and I were real good pool players, but I always told people I was better. But that was just a joke I like to play on him. The truth was Faye could really shoot some pool too. We were very competitive, and we always bet big. That night I won $1600.00 from a guy and then quit while I was ahead. I went back to my room to rest up for the long drive home the next day. But Faye recalls it a little differently. He says I went back to my room with $1600.00 and the guy's girlfriend. Most likely, his version is the way it went down!

My door was still open and I saw that guy I'd just beat running down the hall towards my room waving a gun at me yelling loudly he wants his money back. I slammed the door and got it locked just in time, but he was able to fire off two shots. Both of them went through the door and one grazed the side of my head. Faye rushed me to Parkland Memorial Hospital where they patched me up with several stitches. As I was recovering in the ER the doctor came in and said I was very lucky—a half inch lower and I'd be lying over in that room next door dead. That was the same room where they took President Kennedy just a few months before. I just couldn't believe I was in the same hospital with a gunshot wound to my head, in the same operating room, with the same doctor, in the same year that President Kennedy was shot.

This next adventure I get a laugh at now although it was frightening at the time, a group of four of us was traveling through Alabama on the Southern Swing Tour. It was a long day of driving, and we were hot and thirsty, so when we came into a small town we stopped for gas.

I filled up the car and went to the "colored" bathroom. Then I went inside and asked the attendant where the colored folks hung out in that town. We wanted to go out, have a few beers, and play some pool.

He said, "Boy, take a walk around the corner and you'll see that big ol' tree we got over there. Last colored I saw in this town was hanging from it."

Well, needless to say, we left and found another town to stay in that night.

CHAPTER 3

Where It All Began

New Orleans, Louisiana is where I was born on March 9, 1937. Our home was halfway between the New Orleans Country Club and the Metairie Country Club. I can still remember that street today, and those old shotgun houses are still there. Of course much of the neighborhood has since been remodeled several times, but whenever I go back there for a visit, it still brings back memories of my childhood.

The Metairie Country Club was one of the finest golf courses of its time. It was like no other and attracted golfers from all over. My dad was a caddie there, and he taught my brothers and me the basics of how to caddie. Fred Haas Sr. was the head, pro and his son Fred Haas Jr. would go on to have five wins on the PGA Tour and one win on The Champions Tour. This was the place where he got his start.

When I was about eight years old I started going to the golf courses with my brother Felton (or Faye as everybody called him) after school and on weekends to shag balls. You see, back then they didn't have tractors to go out on the range and collect the balls, so we would shag them, or run out and retrieve them, for the golfer we were working for. And we would only pick up his balls. The faster we could shag, the more money we could make. I usually would make sixty to seventy cents a day, sometimes as much as a dollar, and that was good money back then. When I turned ten I was shagging for a guy named Ben Hogan. He really liked my speed and determination, and he was always working on his hook. That's what he fought with the most—that hook. He said it's like a rattlesnake in your pocket. Finally he was able to perfect that hook into a controlled fade consistently. I guess he saw something in me, because he always paid me three dollars. We worked long days until it was so dark I couldn't find the balls anymore.

Back in those days they didn't have tournaments like they have today. They had exhibitions. There was no prize money, but the club paid the pros to come out and play an exhibition. Fred Jr. knew all the top players, and they all wanted to play there and compete so Fred Jr. easily persuaded the best players to come to Metairie for exhibitions. One Wednesday when I was shagging balls for Mr. Hogan, I knew there was an exhibition starting the following day. I asked him to let me caddie the event for him. Mr. Hogan asked me if I could handle carrying that big ol' leather Burton bag. I was only ten and, boy, were those bags heavy. I told him I would carry two of them if he would let me.

I was tall and strong for my age, and I was determined and confident enough to handle anything. I caddied for Mr. Hogan on Thursday, Friday, Saturday, and Sunday in a threesome that included Sam Snead and Freddy Haas Jr. Ben Hogan paid me five dollars each day, and for a boy my age back then that was a lot of money. After that, Ben always asked me to caddie for him when he came back to town. That was a real honor for a boy my age, and I knew I had earned the respect of my dad and the other caddies because of my relationship with Ben.

Mr. Hogan was the first professional golfer I ever worked for as a professional caddie. He is the person that first took me under his wing and showed me how to caddie the right way. He was very good at explaining things properly and was always a very kind gentleman. The first thing I learned from Ben Hogan was to never touch the grip of the club when I handed it to him. You see the grips are leather, and his sweat gets on them. They could get very wet on a hot summer day, and the last thing a golfer needs is to have a club slip from his hand. It was my job to keep the grips dry, and if I touched them then my sweat would get on the grip too. That was real important and still is today, even with all the new technology.

The next time you watch the pros on TV, you'll notice that the caddies don't touch the grips. It had nothing to do with me being black and him being white, some folks would think that. Mr. Hogan was a very respectful man, and back then all the caddies were black. Now days you only see white caddies on the tour.

One day, on the seventh hole, Mr. Hogan hit the ball out of bounds. He told me, "You can't catch a coon with the dog tied up." I wondered what he meant by that, but rule number one for being a good caddie is you never talk to the pro unless he asks you a question. So I waited until we got to the 9th hole where we would get a drink of water and take a little break.

"What did that mean back on the 7th hole?" I said. "You can't catch a coon with the dog tied up?"

He smiled. "It just means you have to follow through with the club rather than just take a swing at the ball; you have to release the club."

I'll tell you why that became very important to me later on in my career with Gary Player.

My first tournament win was in 1960 with Tony Lema. The prize money was $25,000 and that was a lot of money back then. A lot of folks think that a caddie automatically gets 10% of the winnings. Well that's a myth. Golfers don't have to pay you any part of their winnings if they don't want to, but it's usually between 5% and 10% plus a weekly salary.

Not one single pro I worked for ever gave me any golf lessons. Believe it or not we learned how to play on our own after school, and we learned the rules on our own too.

In New Orleans, Mondays were caddie days. It was the only day of the week we were allowed play golf, and we could only play with the other caddies. But we managed to get in some extra play. When we weren't shagging balls after school, when there was still a little daylight, we'd sneak onto the Metairie golf course over on to the front nine by the railroad tracks, and we'd play holes four, five, six, and seven.

There were usually about five of us kids, and we shared one club. When the greens keeper would come out to catch us on the golf course, we'd run across the canal. If they caught us, they'd take us in the back room and give our ass a whipping with a cat o' nine tails. And then we'd get another whipping when we got home. That's another reason I was fast.

That's how we learned. Every evening we'd sneak onto the course and go play golf. It kept us out of trouble and off the streets too, so Metairie Country Club and New Orleans Country club is where I learned to play golf and caddie.

I'm sure that most of the people I caddied for on those two courses are no longer with us, but I wonder if they'd let me play there now if they knew that's where I got my start. Wouldn't that be great? My brother Felton, and Louis Stewart who I grew up with, and I all caddied on the tour together and this is where we learned the game.

My dad was a caddie there at Metairie and the New Orleans Country Club too, and he was a big part of how we got our start. I learned a lot from him. He even caddied for Gary Player before I did. We had to earn our own money because there were eight kids in my family, so we all had to learn to pay our own way at a very young age, and we all took care of my mother.

When I was older I moved to California, and I would take any job I could get when I wasn't caddying. I used to work at the Golden Bird Chicken Company delivering fried chickens and French fries. This was the best chicken you ever tasted. It was like a Popeye's now days, but it was huge in Los Angeles back then. People would call up and say they needed twenty chickens for a picnic or party. My boss paid me twenty-five cents per chicken. That doesn't sound like a lot of money, but at that time those quarters would add up. When I added that money to what I made caddying, I could afford to travel during the season and still send my mother money every month.

CHAPTER 4

Nickname

A lot of folks think that I got my nickname from Hogan because I was quick like a rabbit and could shag balls faster than anyone else with my bare hands. Creamy Caroline sometimes used a baseball glove. That was very entertaining for the other caddies and golfers. And the fans loved it.

My nickname actually was given to me by my basketball coach, Father Dyney. In high school I played basketball for Saint Joan of Arc Roman Catholic School. One day our center was injured and couldn't play. So Father Dyney told me to take the position at center. He told me to just go out there and jump like a rabbit. We won the basketball conference tournament, and from then on my name was Rabbit.

There were a lot of us with nicknames, and I think it just became a tradition. There was really never any rhyme or reason behind it. Some of the more popular caddie names you have probably heard of are Fluff, Creamy, Golfball, Puzzle, Hobo, Mitch, Texas Sam and Killer Sam.

John Downing

Rabbit summer 2012

CHAPTER 5

Life on the Road

Black Knight International Archives

1973 Westchester Classic

After we started caddying for the pros we would follow them from tournament to tournament down south. On the Southern Swing Tour we would take a Greyhound or we'd all pile into one or two cars and drive all night to the next tournament. Sometimes we slept in our cars or a van, and we change clothes in the woods or parking lot in the morning before the tournament. We weren't allowed in the clubhouse back then. When we could afford it we shared a hotel room, and if one of us had a good week we shared our winnings with the other caddies. We stuck together on the road. We were a tight group, and still are till the end. I've even buried a caddie whose family couldn't afford to. That's just how close we were—a band of brothers.

There are those who think that the pros took us with them and paid our expenses. Not in those days. The caddie's today travel by jets, and sports cars are not uncommon as bonuses. These new caddies can make more money in one tournament than we made in a year—when they're winning of course. Now days there are more white caddies than black caddies, and most of them are college graduates. I can‘t remember seeing a black caddie on the tour lately. Some caddies today are PGA professionals caddying for Tour pro's, sons and daughters carrying for moms and dads, wives and husbands carrying the bags for their spouses. Today anyone can caddie if the pro wants you on his bag. There are caddie courses and schools out there, but no real requirements. I was just watching a tournament on TV when a caddie was overcome by heatstroke and the player was in the lead. The player asked if anyone in the gallery wanted to carry his bag. A young college kid came down from the stands and took his bag, and they won the tournament. I wonder if he got 10% and is paid a salary now, driving a sports car and flying jets to the next tournament. It could happen. Boy, a lot sure has changed since I started as a kid.

I remember when Jack Nicklaus hired Angelo Argea. We were in Las Vegas. Angelo was a good caddie, and he drove a cab part time to supplement his income. We were getting ready for the Las Vegas Open, and Jack came in and asked the caddie master if he had a caddie for him for the next day. The caddie master said they were all taken but one, and he would call Angelo in. Angelo came in the next day and caddied for Jack. Jack won, and Angelo quit his cab job and became Jacks permanent caddie for many, many years.

Back in 1974 the rules for the PGA Championship stated that the golfer must use an assigned caddie, so I wasn't allowed to caddie in that tournament for Gary Player. We had just won the British Open and The Masters only allowed club caddies, and if I'd been able to caddie Winged Foot at the US Open we'd have been playing for a Grand Slam that year. Well another caddie was assigned, and he had never caddied a professional golf tournament before. His name was Clarence Simmington. He was actually a tobacco worker, believe it or not.

So I went ahead and walked the course in the morning to get the yardages and pin placements, and I gave all of this information to Gary ahead of time. So all Clarence really had to do was carry the bag and hand Gary the club. I also told him that Gary sometimes got really wound up, and you have to calm him down. And every now and then he goes into such a focused state of concentration that you have to wake him up. I could have walked the course on the other side of the ropes with the gallery, but I chose to watch it from the ABC truck instead. Lee Trevino ended up winning with Jack Nicklaus just one stroke behind. Gary finished even at seventh place. Not too bad for a man with two caddies that week.

Black Knight International Archives

1976 PGA Championship practice

AP Wire Service

Player using field worker as PGA caddie

CLEMMONS, N.C. (AP) –"Keep the balls and clubs clean and keep your mouth shut." That was the advice passed on to Clarence Simmington, Gary Player's caddie, Tuesday by Alfred (Rabbit) Dyer, the third member of the unique triumvirate bidding this weekend for the South African's third, major golf championship' of the year–the PGA. "I told him also to be sure and not let our man go to sleep out there," Dyer added. "Gary–he gets to concentrating so hard that he sometimes goes' to sleep, and you got to wake him up." The man they call Rabbit is the stringbean black from New Orleans who kept whispering in Player's ear when the 37-year-old Johannesburg pro added the British Open to his Masters triumph last month in Lytham and St. Anne's, England. Under club rules which state that the player must use the caddie he is assigned, Dyer is not permitted to carry Player's' clubs in the PGA Championship, starting Thursday over the Tanglewood course.

That job has been assigned to Simmington, a tobacco worker who has never caddied for a pro before. "I'll always be in the wings, giving Clarence advice," Rabbit said. "You might say we are a three-man team. "I've already charted the course. Every morning I will get up and check the pin placements. I will pass on this information to Gary. All this" new boy has to do is hand Gary the club. "You don't have to club Gary. All you have to do is slow him down when he gets too charged up and wake him up when he gets into that hypnotic state he talks about." Dyer, who has been Player's tour caddie for 12 years, said he didn't plan to follow his man around the course, although he could do so as a member of the gallery. Instead, he will hold down a job in the ABC-TV

AP Wire Service

trailer. He admitted he was concerned. "If I could have caddied for Gary in the U.S. Open at Winged Foot, there's no doubt we would have won and would have been going for the Grand Slam this week," Dyer said. "My man is the best golfer in the world. You just got to keep him steady. He gets lost in his thoughts—he concentrates so hard."

Player and Rabbit first became a team at the New Orleans Open in 1962. The gangling, 6-foo't4 native of the jazz capital caddied for the South African spasmodically during the next few years while also accompanying such players as Tony Lema, Dave Stockton and Dan Sikes to tour victories.

"Two years ago at Oakland Hills (Birmingham, Mich.), I told Gary he was going to win the PGA there and he did," Rabbit said, "He asked me to caddie for him in the World Series of Golf. I did. We won again. "I knew he was going to win the Masters this year. Then at Memphis, we were five shots behindwith 11 holes to play. I told Gary 'Go out and shoot a 32 on the back nine and we'll win. He shot a 31 and won." Dyer, who wears a wide brimmed plantation sombrero and dark glasses, says Player's forte as a golfer is his mind.

"He is smarter than everybody else," the caddie contended. "He knows how to play safe. He knows how and when to gamble. He is always ready." At Lytham and St. Anne's, according to Rabbit, Player concentrated so intensely that he kept asking the caddie how he stood. "I told him I'd tell him at the 17th," Dyer said. "At the 17th, even after bogeying, I told Gary he had five shots to spare. Like a jockey on a race horse, I said, 'Okay, Gary, now go get 'em,' and he did.

CHAPTER 6

"They saw the black face, not the heart of the man"

Black Knight International Archives

African Open Championship

In 1974 when I went to South Africa it was bad over there—real bad being a black man over there then. That was it. You had to stand up and stand your ground. It was not a good place to be if you were in my shoes, but we had to break some barriers somehow and earn our respect. The government's ways were all about whites with whites, blacks with blacks, and Indians with Indians. It was rough, and things needed to change.

Well, Gary told me I could stay with him at his ranch. I thanked him, but I told him I wanted to stay downtown so I could see the sights and be around the people. I got a room at the Holiday Inn, Millpark. The car I had over there was a Volkswagen Gulf, and I would go from town to town, meeting the people of different communities and cultures on my off days. Then I would meet Gary and caddie at the tournaments. I was always welcomed at his ranch and at Fulton Allem's place to be safe. I would often travel into Soweto. That was a pretty dangerous place, and we were advised by the government not to go there. But I wanted to go in there and try to make a difference and help those people. I made some friends, and I think I made a difference as well.

I wanted to be on my own over there as much as possible. This car I was driving at the time had a steering wheel on the right side, and in the passenger seat I had this little chick. She was my interpreter. At one point a guy pulled up next to me on this big motorcycle. He started kicking the car door yelling, "You caffer! You cut me off, you caffer!"

Black Knight International Archives

1981 South African Open Championship

My interpreter asked me if I knew what caffer meant. When I told her no, she said told me it was the same as calling someone a nigger in America.

The man was still kicking the door. "Get out of the car, caffer," he said.

Everywhere I'd gone in South Africa I'd seen that most black people there were small. This guy just saw me sitting in the car and had no idea how big I was. By the time I stood up out of the car it was too late for him to do anything. It only took me two licks, and he was out cold. His motorcycle fell one way, and he went down the other.

My interpreter told me I couldn't do that.

I shrugged and slipped back in behind the wheel of the car. "I'm an American," I said. "I got the blue passport. They can't do nothing to me. Besides, he started it."

What I didn't know at the time was that there were a couple of golfers on the same street just a few cars back. The next day they came over to me at the tournament. They said they saw me knock that guy out. Then they shook my hand. I told them I was just defending myself, and we all started laughing. I for sure earned their respect, but I wasn't too popular at first with some of the locals. I must have gotten into seven or eight fights over there.

When I was there the next year, in 1975, I wanted to take a friend on a tour of a game reserve. Fulton Allem loaned me his Mercedes for a few days. He was a South African golfer who was a close friend of Gary's. He won eleven times on the Sunshine Tour and at least twice on the PGA Tour. He had some health issues and retired early but still plays on the Champions Tour. He now lives in Florida a few miles from Jim Thorpe, and just an hour from me.

But the thing was, you just didn't see a black man driving a Mercedes in South Africa back then. Only policemen and chauffeurs drove Mercedes. If you didn't have a uniform and were black you were a sure target to be pulled over. It didn't take too long before I was spotted at a roba (what they call a red light) by two cops on motorcycles. They followed us for a while, and then stopped us. That's when the policeman recognized the car, and then they saw how tall I was.

One cop turned to the other. "I know who that is," he said. "That's Rabbit, Gary Player's caddie."

"Oh, yeah," said his partner with a big smile. "Let's take him down town to the police station to meet the chief."

So I followed them and went inside to meet the chief of police and a few other policemen. We talked, and I told them how much I liked being in their country. They asked me questions about golf and wanted tips and advice on improving their games. I don't really think they had ever picked up a club, but I went along with it anyway to be nice. After all, it was the chief of police. We had something to eat for lunch and had a good ol' time. I gave them all golf balls. There was no ticket, no hassle, nothing. And I never had any problems again being pulled over in South Africa.

I was the first black American to caddie over on the South African tour, and the other tour caddies from Europe and South Africa didn't like that too much. We won the South African Masters and the South African PGA, so if you count those, then I would have been the first caddie to have a grand slam.

Black Knight International Archives

1981 South African Open Championship

Lee Elder was the first black American golfer to play in South Africa. Gary invited him to come out to help bridge the color barrier in the game of golf. He was tremendously proud of that. Lee Elder competing in South Africa really opened a lot of doors for South African golfers. It did a lot for their self confidence, and it raised awareness over there and also raised a lot of money for South African schools. It created a new surge of encouragement, and soon after, there were more black South African golfers on the tour than there had ever been before. I heard there were more than fifty in just one year to become pro.

Lee Elder and I had gone to a Pro Am party together at one of the South African tournaments. We saw Arnold Palmer over by the casino with Tom Weiskopf, Dave Stockton, Bobby Locke, and Fulton Allem. When we walked over to say hello to them a Dutch golfer, Vince Baker, confronted us.

"Hey, you caffer," he yelled, looking right at me. "What are you doing? Caddies can't go in there."

That's when Arnold Palmer stood up and told him to leave me alone.

Baker had no clue I was a welter weight champ, and could take him out with one punch if I wanted to. But I didn't want to cause any trouble, and this guy sure was trying to start some.

I turned and headed out, just wanting to go back to my room and relax. But Baker followed me down the hallway. That was the biggest mistake he ever made. I could see he just wanted to make trouble, so I finished it before it even started. I knocked him on his butt with one punch right there in the hallway. He struggled to his feet with a look of shock on his face, then he ran back the way he'd come.

I heard the rest of the story from some of the guys later on. Baker came running into the casino and headed for Arnold Palmer. "Arnold," he yelled. "Rabbit just punched me!"

Arnold shook his head. "I told you to leave Rabbit alone, but you just wouldn't listen would you? Don't mess with Rabbit. I hope you learned your lesson."

That Dutchman didn't know how well I could fight. Like I said, black men over there tended to be smaller than me. And growing up the way I did, I had to learn to fight, and I was good at it. I wasn't proud at all about the fights I was in, but with the apartheid and all the attitudes that went with it, I felt I had to defend myself and never look weak.

The most publicized fight I was ever in was at the British Open. This was the fight heard around the world. I was the first black man to caddie over there in its 102-year-history, and there was a lot of controversy over that. In some ways, the British Open was like a mini version of South Africa. The Dutchmen and Englishmen thought they should be the only ones to caddie, not blacks. So I was out getting my yardage one evening at about seven when it was still daylight. All of a sudden three Dutch caddies approached me, yelling at me to go home to America. They said they didn't want me there and threatened to kick my ass before Sunday. I just ignored them and kept walking, minding my own business and continuing to get my yardage for the next day. I had a lot of people watching me, there was always a small gallery of two or three hundred people following me and watching me work before and after the rounds. Well these three caddies got closer and closer and started poking me in my back with a golf club. They made a big mistake when two of them went back into the clubhouse and left Oosterhuis' caddie, a Dutchman, alone out there with me. The next day the headlines in the newspaper read, "American caddie 'Sugar Ray Rabbit' knocks Dutch caddie out on the 17th green."

Most people over there, however, were nice once they saw that I was American. Some just saw the black face and couldn't see the heart of the man, and that is still true today. It's sad.

CHAPTER 7

A Fly in Buttermilk

1974 British Open

AP Wire Service

Player brings black caddie

LYTHAM ST. ANNE'S, England

(AP) – Gary Player, the golfing star from racially conscious South Africa, has

Shown up at (he British Open Championship with a black caddie from New Orleans. "I don't care if he's a South African, all I know is he's a gentleman,"

6-foot-4 Alfred "Rabbit" Dyer, the caddie from the South, said Monday.

Dyer, 36, held court for enthralled golf fans at the clubhouse door Mondayas he waited to join Player in a practice round over the grim old course.

"He's the best caddie I ever had in my life," Player said. Dyer, who now lives in East Orange, N.J., naturally picks Player to win his third British Open.

"Gary has all the equipment to beat this course," the caddie said. "He drives straight, he plays out of the traps like a dream, and he's a great putter.

"1 first caddied for Gary at the New Orleans Open in 1962, and I've never known him in such good form. "He's going to win, man."

Dyer claims he caddied for 12 winners in his career, including Dave Stockton, Sam Snead, Doug Sanders and the late Tony Lema. Dyer, who says he earned his nickname because he jumped like a rabbit in his basketball days at college, set off a minor furor with his appearance as Player's caddie from across the Atlantic.

AP Wire Service

Player's former caddie here, Al Fyles was upset. He and Player argued noisily in front of the clubhouse." My grouse is that Gary never let me know he was bringing this other fellow," Fyles said. "I feel a bit hurt." Fyles worked for Player in five Piccadilly World Match Play triumphs at Wentworth, near London, between 1965 and1973 and threw his cap in the air when the South African won the British Open at Carnoustie, Scotland, in 1968.

The fast-talking Dyer said he plans to accompany Player to South Africa next year. "If they try to restrict me there, it's going to be too bad for them," he said.

"Whatever anyone says about Gary Player, no one man can make a country."

Dyer was asked if he felt out of place as a black caddie in a tournament where the caddies traditionally are wizened Scotsmen with little to say. "I suppose I'm different," Dyer said. "I guess I look like a fly in a glass of buttermilk."

AP Wire Photo via cable from London

1974 British Open

Gary was always kind and looked out for me better than anyone did. Not that I needed to be looked after, but there were a lot more color issues back then with segregation in America, apartheid in South Africa, and breaking the color barrier in Royal Lytham & St. Annes to caddie in The British Open. Gary asked me to always make sure I'm wearing my badge at the tournament.

"Relax," I said. "I'll be fine. You know I stand out like a fly in buttermilk. There aren't any other black men around here as big as me. I don't need a badge."

He laughed. And still tells that story, even today.

"People have always called me the best golfer of those who traveled all over the world," Player said at Lytham. "What I've worked so hard to become is one of the best golfers in the world, period."

He was that, and more, at Lytham. Fit as always and remarkably confident, he shot rounds of 69, 68, 75 and 70 for 282, and simply wouldn't allow anyone to beat him. "I'm playing the best golf of my life," he said—not that he hasn't said the same a hundred other times. But what he added was not so familiar, and probably right: "I've never been as well prepared. I can't believe anyone else is as ready for this as I am—or wants it as badly."

The only other person who might have been was Player's caddie, the inimitable Alfred Dyer, he of the plantation hat. Known as Rabbit, he started off the week getting as many headlines as Player and signing as many autographs. He was the first black caddie in the British Open. That's one thing. The other thing was, the British thought Rabbit was funny.

"My man complains a lot," said Rabbit one day. "I just stick some paper in my ears, and say, 'Don't gimme no jive, baby,' and I make him laugh, loosen him up." Rabbit occasionally caddies for Player in the States but never abroad. "He's the best caddie I've ever had," Gary said. "He knows distances and he knows me."

Sports Illustrated
SI Vault July 22 1974
Dan Jenkins

The weather at that tournament can be fine one minute and brutal the next. The wind can change in a split second, and the temperature can drop several degrees at any time when the sea breeze blows in. The conditions are so unpredictable. That's just the weather. Now imagine playing on one of the oldest and most prestigious courses in the world. There are no trees, but there are tall grasses that run along the edge of the fairways. Then there are those deep thick bunkers. Many of them are grass bunkers and rough that will tear your pants leg. They say there are over two hundred of them. The grass bunkers over there aren't at all like sand bunkers in the US. The ones over there are called pot bunkers, and they're made of tall, thick grass. Before we started the tournament Gary told me that was the one place he did not want to hit the ball, or it would be big trouble.

We had a six shot lead going into the 71st hole. We had a long rough and Gary's shot landed in one of those thick, grass pot bunkers where no one could see it unless you were looking right down on it. The ball landed in the exact area Gary didn't want it to go. We were both confident that if we didn't find the ball, he would still have an easy victory, even with the penalty. But we did find it.

As he was about to hit the shot out of that bunker, Gary leaned towards me with a smile on his face and asked if I thought we could win from here.

I returned his smile. "Man, Ray Charles could win from here," I said.

We bogeyed 17 and moved on to 18 where Gary's second shot landed two inches from the clubhouse wall, and about twenty feet from the pin. There were thousands of spectators closing in, and there were people hanging out of windows right above Gary's ball. The only way to putt that ball would be left handed. Otherwise he'd have had to take a penalty and drop. Gary thought and focused. He even had to tell the man who was looking out the window of the clubhouse to please quiet down so he could concentrate. It was chaos on that final hole for certain. Gary approached the ball, turned his putter upside down, and gently, left handed, hit it to within a few feet of the pin. Then he tapped it in for one of the most memorable British Open's in history, and a four shot win over Peter Oosterhuis with Jack Nicklaus just five back.

Now, I've heard all of the "conspiracy theories," and it still comes up to this day about that lost ball at St. Annes 1974. Every year, a week or two before The British Open and the week following, it truly seems like I get twenty or thirty requests for interviews about that final round in 1974. I do the interviews still, but I think from now on I'm going to have to start charging for them, especially at my age. Maybe this book will be it and the "conspiracy theory" will go away for good. I've heard them all, and it doesn't bother me anymore, because I know what truly happened, and that was the marshal found the ball with time left on the clock. Gary made sure they had the stopwatch on him. I've heard that the ball was found later

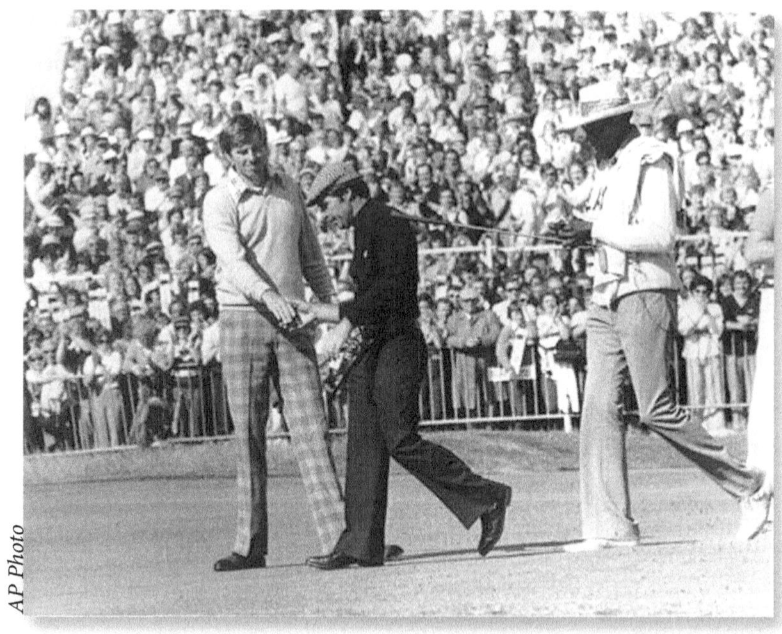

AP Photo

1974 British Open Peter Oosterhuis, Gary Player and Rabbit Dyer

and hidden in a secret safe at Royal Laytham & St. Annes and is still there to this day. I've heard I had a secret pocket in my pants, just in case of this situation, and I could let the seam out and the ball would fall from my pants leg. A ball was hidden in my shoe, or there was an identical ball that was right where I was standing and he hit a lost ball. I read that someone in the gallery found the ball and kept it as a souvenir. Come on! How many stories are there? Did I miss any?

Now let's look at this. I was being watched by millions of people on TV. We had photographers with zoom lenses all over us. I had Oosterhuis' caddie and the marshals searching with me. Not to mention the thousands of spectators watching in front of and behind me. Now don't you think that since we were at the 17th hole with no groups behind us, that maybe someone who had doubts would have sent a search team out to look for that ball? What about the next day? Plus each player has a special mark on their golf balls to identify them, and they are numbered. Well, where it is now?

CHAPTER 8

Gary Player

Black Knight International Archives

1975 Kemper Open

My father had caddied for Gary Player just two years before me in 1960. Two years later, in 1962, I caddied for him the first time when he came to New Orleans for a tournament. Back then all the golfers names were put into a grab bag or a hat, and the caddies would draw the names. Whoever you drew, that's who you caddied for. I drew Gary Player's name out of the hat, so I caddied for him that tournament. He came in fifth place and paid me $300.00. That was the most money I had ever made at one time. I never saw that kind of money.

I didn't see Gary for ten years after that. In 1972 I was driving a truck and working as an independent contractor for ABC television. I drove the ABC truck from tournament to tournament with the set for Howard Cosell and other sporting events. I loaded, unloaded, and set up the sets and graphics.

I had just arrived in Birmingham, Michigan, at Oakland IIills for the PGA Championship and was working on thc set when Gary spotted me and walked over. "Hey, aren't you Rabbit?" he said.

I smiled and shook his hand. "Yeah, I caddied for you ten years ago in New Orleans."

I asked him, if he won the PGA tournament that week, who was going to caddie for him in the World Series of Golf the following week. In those days if you played the PGA, The British Open, The US Open, and the Masters you got invited to the World Series of Golf. The PGA was the last leg before the World Series of Golf which at the time was an exhibition tournament that Gary Player first won in 1965. The World Series of Golf is now a sanctioned PGA tournament renamed The Bridgestone Invitational.

"Rabbit," he said. "If you have that much faith in me, and I win this PGA, then you got yourself a job next week, because my caddie is going back to South Africa after this tournament, and I need a good caddie."

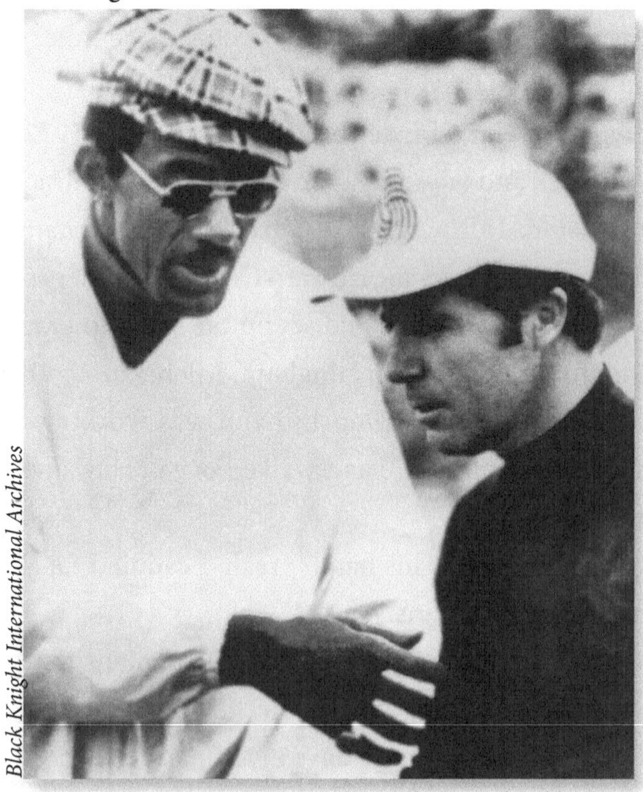

Black Knight International Archives

Gary Player and Rabbit Dyer

That was the beginning, and I stayed with him until 1992. I've seen articles that I caddied for him for eighteen years. I am not exactly sure where they came up with that number. Actually it was for twenty years, from 1972 to 1992. But my best explanation for the error is that Gary won the British Open in 1974, and that was a big tournament for the record books, so people took note of me being his caddie. But I started with him in 1972 at the World Series of Golf.

We still see each other about once a year. When hurricane Katrina hit, I was living in New Orleans. Gary called me and asked if I was alright. I told him I'd just lost everything—my pictures, my memorabilia, and my clothes. A few days later Gary arranged for me to get a whole new wardrobe, and he paid for it all. Now that is a nice man.

Water—that was one thing Gary didn't like to be around. When we were close to water he would say, "How are we going to get through that water?"

I would look right at it and say, "Water? Where? What water? I don't see no water!"

We would laugh, and that would loosen him back up. That's a big part of being a caddie—to keep the golfer loose and focused, not worrying about what could happen but helping him do what needs to happen with no mistakes.

Gary Player still has an incredible career. He is an international golfer and is still called the most traveled athlete. I caddied eighteen US PGA tournaments a year for twenty years, so that's 360 tournaments, not including the Irish Tour and the South African Tour. So I'd say just caddying for Gary, we were in over five hundred professional tournaments. He has 165 victories over five decades and around sixty-eight with me carrying his bag. He's one of only three players in history to win the British Open in three different decades and the third player in history to have a career Grand Slam.

Gary had an incredible attitude and outlook on life. He always felt he was blessed and that golf was a gift from God to him. He always kept in mind that just as he received that gift, it could be taken away just as fast. He was always positive and his work ethic was like no other. He was a strong man but small. He weighed 150 pounds and could bench press three hundred. Believe me, I used to drive the van with all of his weights and workout equipment in it from tournament to tournament. He would always challenge other golfers out on the driving range to hold a driver between their first and third fingers at the grip and balance it parallel to the ground. If they could—only a few could—he would grab a wood and a driver and do it with two clubs. I never saw anybody else do that with two clubs. I bet after you read this you will be going straight over to your bag for your driver. Give it a shot. You'll see how strong he was.

Gary was all about being fit, healthy, and strong. He said being in shape wasn't just about your physical shape, but your mental shape as well. He saw me with a cigarette early on, and he told me choose that or choose caddying. I never smoked ever again.

Gary had very strong principles and beliefs too. He was always very faithful, committed, focused, and determined. Every round he played, no matter what the challenge or level of difficulty was, he convinced himself that he was going to win. When asked how he could make those putts to win championships on the 18th hole he would say, "I simply tell myself I'm going to make that putt. I've practiced that putt hundreds of times and made it, so the odds are I will make it this time."

Gary treated me very well, and he was always respectful to me. He even called me this year on his 77th birthday from Singapore just to talk and see how my book was coming along and to ask I was doing in my new place here in Florida.

When it was time to send my son to college, Gary gave me $100,000 to send him to Princeton University. He would give me $20,000 at a time, and I always made sure that when he won I would pay him back the money I owed him, Gary made sure of that too this must have been motivating for Gary to win so much, to insure my loans would be paid back quickly!

CHAPTER 9

Celebrities & Presidents

Bob Hope

Alfred Rabbit Dyer

Jack Whitacker and Rabbit Dyer

I lived in Los Angeles for four years. While I was there I used to caddie at the El Caballero Country Club, the Los Angeles Country Club, the Riviera Country Club. I caddied for all those clubs out there.

One day Bob Hope came in and I got his bag. After that day, he requested that I caddie for him in the Bob Hope Classic. We got along real good, and whenever I wasn't caddying for Gary Player, I'd go to California and caddie for Bob Hope. At the country club, if you were next in line, that's who you caddied for. But Bob Hope always asked for me, so the draw didn't matter to me, because I always know I would get him. The only time I didn't caddie for him in the Bob Hope Classic was when Gary Player was playing in it. Of course, I was always Gary's caddie first.

Bob Hope used to play with a lot of celebrities, Billy Eckstein (he was a singer), Sidney Poitier, Joe Lewis quite often. They had a lot of fun with each other, but they played serious golf. No fooling around. They had a few dollars on the table. Bob Hope was good. He was about a five or six handicap. Sometimes he and his friends would have side bets, off the table, and they were rumored to be between $50,000 and $100,000. Bob was very generous and gave me a solid gold golf bag on a gold chain that I still wear every day.

Alfred Rabbit Dyer

Lee Trevino and Rabbit

After I caddied for Bob hope a few years, I caddied for Evel Knievel. We would go to Butte, Montana, and he'd put us up in this beautiful hotel for a week. I was like a fly in buttermilk in Butte if anywhere. There were very few blacks in that town in those days. You see, Evel Knievel had class, and he couldn't have just one caddie. He always had three caddies—a caddie named Sam "Killer" Foy, Toby, and me. He would have Toby drive the cart, Killer would serve the drinks, and I would do the actual caddying. In 1976 he invited the three of us to the Bicentennial parade out there. He was the grand marshal, and was also unveiling his sky rocket to jump over Snake River Canyon. We got all dressed up in our black pants and silk shirts and rode on the float, and we were all waving at the crowd. I heard his son, Robbie, is now living close by here in Florida. He was a good kid. I'd like to see him again and say hi someday.

I caddied for a lot of celebrities. They were all real nice. Frank Sinatra was very nice to me. I caddied for him in a tournament down in Canyon Country Club in Palm Springs a few times. He had a tournament there. I caddied for Billy

Eckstein and Sidney Poitier in Los Angeles, and for Sammy Davis Jr. at his tournament in Hartford Connecticut, and in California a couple times.

I caddied for so many people. Here are some of the most memorable:

Pete Brown, Allen Miller, Mark Lyle, Calvin Pete, Lee Trevino, Arnold Palmer, Gary Player, Chi Chi Rodriguez, Raymond Floyd, Jim Dent, Calvin Peete, Tony Lema, Fulton Allem, Jim Thorpe, Ben Hogan, Sam Snead, Dan Sykes, Lee Elder, Charlie Sifford, Dave Stockton, Fred Haas, Bobby Locke, Billy Eckstein, Sidney Poitier, Bob Hope, Sammy Davis Jr., Joe Lewis, Frank Sinatra, Mickey Rooney, Dinah Shore, Tip O'Neill, General Chaffy James, President Ford, President Eisenhower, Alan Sheppard, Mickey Rooney, Babe Zaharias, and Dean Martin.

Alfred Rabbit Dyer

Rabbit and Arnold Palmer

CHAPTER 10

Chi Chi Rodriguez

A Great Friend

Alfred Rabbit Dyer

Rabbit and Chi Chi Rodriguez

I caddied for Chi Chi about forty or fifty times. He loved to dress colorfully, and he could really drive the ball straight and far. He also loved to play and joke around. He was a real entertainer. He was a show off to the gallery and had a lot of trick shots he would do for them. His favorite move was the sword move after he would make a putt. I just saw him at the PGA Show this year, and he and his wife are doing great!

John Downing

Chi Chi Rodriguez, Mark Lye from the Golf Channel and Rabbit

CHAPTER 11

Presidents & Dignitaries

President Eisenhower had a house on the El Dorado Country Club. When I was caddying there one day, the caddie master come up to me and asked me to caddie for Eisenhower. He knew I would do a good job. So from then on when I was there Eisenhower always requested me. He was a very nice guy.

The security there was tight, but caddying for a president back then was different than it is today. On the course there are a lot of big garbage cans. In the old days, before we started, they would fill those garbage cans up with water in case there were any explosives planted in them. Now most of the golf courses are fenced in, and no one can sneak in through the woods. But even then you would see Secret Service hiding back in the woods and following us real close. Eisenhower would tell me, "Enjoy yourself. You're not out there with them; you're out here with me." That was the safest I ever felt though. They were out there with big ol' guns and everything.

I caddied for President Ford in North Carolina. He was a real nice person too, he wasn't the greatest golfer, and even though he really enjoyed playing, I'd have to say Eisenhower was the better golfer. President Ford pretty much just played to relax and enjoy himself.

Who knows, maybe President Obama will read this. If he sees that I caddied for two presidents, maybe he'll let me caddie for him someday.

Now, how many people can say they've had the opportunity to caddie for so many people of such extraordinary fame, athletic ability, and outstanding quality in their lifetimes?

CHAPTER 12

Caddies

Alfred Rabbit Dyer

Jimmy Clark, Lee Elder and Rabbit Dyer

Caddies now days have sponsors just like the pros. They're endorsing hotels, clubs, shoes—you name it. Usually the caddie's sponsors are the same as the pro they're with, so there's no conflict. Back then we didn't get sponsored for anything. The picture of me standing behind Gary with a La Mode hat on didn't pay me a dime. If I was caddying today with that same hat I'd be a wealthy man.

The caddying days as I knew them are long gone. Technology has made such an impact on the game. The way caddying is done now is more of a science. In my day it was an art. The day before a tournament we would walk the entire course and get the yardage and write it down. We might pick a certain tree, bush, or landmark just so we would have some distances that weren't just from sprinkler heads or yard markers. Now they have GPS and more sophisticated ways of getting yardage. As far as I'm concerned, nothing beats the old fashioned way of good ol' hard work.

In 1974 I won the Melbourne Open Caddie tournament with Lee Trevino's caddie, Herman "Big Mitch" Mitchell. It was a best ball, and we shot a sixty-six. Our prize was a Ping golf bag, a set of Ping golf clubs and $1500.00. I was in Pensacola and was robbed two days later, they took it all, $2000.00 and my golf clubs. I never got to use those Pings.

My brother Faye and I would travel together back in the days before Gary. Faye says he's caddied more years and for more pros than I ever did and jokes often, wondering how I got in the Caddie Hall of Fame and he didn't. We had a van and would travel all over the country together with four or five other caddies. Up North in the late summer and early fall was a good time to caddie in New York, so one fall Faye and I were up there staying in this run down place and working part time in a warehouse between tournaments. Faye was ready to leave New York because it was starting to get cold, and he always hated cold weather. In the winter New York is too cold for a kid from New Orleans. We also knew how to fight too. There were seven boys in my family, and we knew how to fend for ourselves. Well when it started to get cold we only had about $1100.00 between us, and that wasn't enough money to get back to New Orleans. We weren't going to work in that warehouse anymore—it was too dirty and nasty. The boss man was a mean Irishman, and he was always bragging that his son was a Golden Gloves boxer who could whoop both our asses anytime. Faye weighed about 140, and the boss's son was about 210. So I told the boss I would bet all of our $400.00 that Faye could whip the kid. Boss man set up a ring in the warehouse, and I went and got Faye and told him what I did. Faye wasn't too happy about my arrangement, but he knew it was our ticket home. Bets were placed and the money was collected and they went to battle. Well Faye whipped him by about the third round. I mean he was out cold. That boss man got so upset he came after me, and I whipped him in all about two licks. Then the son gets up and takes off his gloves and Faye took off his gloves and we

Caddybytes

Jerry "Hobo" Osborn
(Rabbit's friend for over 40 years, The Humble Hacker)

still whipped their butts again. We collected $1800.00 total and came home to New Orleans each with a pocket full of money.

Being on the road and traveling, we always had all of our money with us in cash. Back then they didn't have ATMs, and we were always on the move. We were targets when people found out who we were. We all knew how to fight, though. We had to in order to protect each other. We all looked out for each other and always stayed in a group. We kept a pistol under the seat of the car for protection too. We had to pull it out a few times but never once used it. Back in those days it was rough being on the road going from city to city, especially in the South.

We got pulled over for speeding quite a bit, but rarely would we get a ticket. We would just tell the police we were caddies trying to get to the next tournament. We always gave them golf balls and told them they were the balls used by a big name pro, and they would let us go. One time Faye and I were driving through Jennings, Louisiana, in a faster sedan when a policeman pulled behind us in one of those checker cars. We looked at each other and smiled, knowing we could easily outrun him. But after a few minutes of discussion we decided to pull over and do the right thing. The policeman asked us what we were up to because we didn't pull over right away. I told him we were discussing outrunning him because our car was much faster than his checkered police car.

"You might be able to outrun this car," he said. "But you can't outrun my radio."

We got a ticket that time. Golf ball payments weren't accepted by this guy. He told us we had to go down to the station. Since we were going twenty miles per hour over the speed limit, he was going to make us talk to the chief. We didn't want him to find the gun we kept under the seat, so we didn't put up a fuss. He let us follow him downtown to the jailhouse to pay a fine in person. When we arrived and the chief asked us why we were in such a hurry, we told him we were caddies and heading to the next tournament. Once he discovered who I was he gave me my license back, tore up the ticket, and sent us on our way.

Afterword

In Gary Player's Words

Transcribed January 25, 2013

"Rabbit caddied for me for plus or minus sixteen or seventeen years, and he was a good friend as well as my caddie. I always called him the Mohammed Ali of golf. He had a smile every day of his life. He had a hearty laugh and was always, always happy. It didn't matter what happened. He had overcome a lot of adversity.

He had a son who we, together, put through Princeton University. It cost Rabbit a lot of money, and I was able to lend him the money without any interest. Rabbit said to me at the time that his son would never appreciate it. I told him of course he would. But his son has never appreciated it, and he should be ashamed of himself that he's never thanked his father and given his father the love he should have. Even though the young man's mother and father didn't get along too well together, whatever the case may be the son should have appreciated it a lot more. So Rabbit did a great thing in sending his son to Princeton—a marvelous thing for a caddie to do that. That's number one.

Number two, he caddied for me in Britain, and he was the first black to caddie and win the British Open, which is the oldest major championship of them all. He was hilarious. I always remember saying, "Listen, you have got to have a badge on when you come into these gates. The police and the security are very tough."

He said, "Don't worry about me, my little brother. I stick out like a fly in buttermilk." I will always remember that expression. When we were doing the press interviews he'd say "we" shot 64, or "we" shot 65. And when I shot 75, then Rabbit would say "he", meaning "me", shot 75. I mean, Rabbit was hilarious.

He came to South Africa in the midst of apartheid, and he contributed whatever he could in his way to eradicate it. What effect his efforts had can't be measured, of course, but he was really good at speaking to people and encouraging them. He's been a wonderful man, a very kind man who loves people. We could be having a tough time in a tournament, and he could always make me laugh.

He would often drive me to the club and tease the woman at the toll gates. He was very much like Mohammed Ali. I remember one occasion we were in front of water and I asked him if he thought I could make it over the water and he said, "What water? I don't see no water." He could always ease any fear with his calmness and sense of humor.

Once, as we were leaving the British Open and getting on the train, I realized we were missing something. He had forgotten the trophy. He went back at five hundred miles an hour to get it. I said, "Oh, can you imagine this?

Here I win this trophy, it's over a hundred years old, and I'm going to be the first one to lose it. They'll hang me on the 18th green!" He went back and he found the trophy.

We were on the 71st hole. I'll never forget, I had a six shot lead. I mean I couldn't lose this tournament, and I hit it in this long rough, right next to the green. We found the ball just in time and managed to get a bogey and we are going down the last hole and I hit my ball over the green. I said, "Do you think we can win from here?"

He said, "Ray Charles could win from here."

It's nice having a six shot lead going into the last two holes, you really can't lose it no matter what happens, and that was very exciting.

I can't say this for a fact, but to the best of my knowledge, yes, he was the first caddie to caddie in all four of the major championships—the Grand Slam of tournaments—which is remarkable.

He always had that big brimmed hat on him, and when he came to South Africa everybody loved him, when we went to Britain everybody loved him, and everywhere we went they were so very fond of him. I just have great memories of him."

Gary Player

Words from Chi Chi Rodriguez

"Rabbit has always been a good friend, on and off the course. He is the most respected caddie to have worked the tour. There isn't a golfer out here that doesn't like and respect Rabbit. He is bigger than life. I talked to Rabbit just the other day and told him, "Mi casa es su casa." He is welcome in my house anytime.

Rabbit is one of the few caddies that had many fans in the gallery follow him. Arnold Palmer and Jack Nicklaus always had a big gallery and so did Rabbit.

We always had a lot of fun, and when Rabbit was around he could really go along with the jokes. He and Jim Thorpe had a lot of fun, and you just couldn't miss Rabbit's big laugh. No one pushed him around either. For one thing, he's 6'4", but the real reason is that he's just a true gentleman. Gary Player was very fortunate to have Rabbit on his bag for as long as he did. There is no one more impressive than Gary Player; he has accomplished more than any other golfer. And to have Rabbit by his side for most of his career should tell you something about Rabbit. He is bigger than life with an even bigger heart."

Chi Chi Rodriguez

Fulton Allem on Rabbit

"I had known Rabbit for quite some time while he was in South Africa working for Gary Player. He's a good friend, salt of the earth. I had known Gary Player as a kid and was encouraged by him and my father to start playing at an early age. I believe I was around seven.

Rabbit is a fantastic, old-school caddie. He really knows how to manage the course and stay focused. When he was considering going back to the US in the mid '80s, I offered to let him stay at my place. And I asked him to caddie for me in 1986 and 1987. It was a great opportunity for me to have a caddie that I could learn from. After all, he had the experience of winning major championships, and, sure enough, we won the 1987 Lexington PGA.

We had a lot of good times off the course too. Rabbit was tough, and nobody over there messed with him. The ones that did weren't standing up too long.

I wish all the best to Rabbit and hope that this book brings him all the joys he deserves in his golden years."

Fulton Allem

John Downing

Rabbit and Kailani Downing

Reflection

Now that I've been able to look back and reflect on my life, I can truly say I lived a full one. I have a permanent place in history and have been able to witness many historical events first hand. In my retirement I plan to continue watching and loving the game. I am hoping soon to start helping kids learn the etiquette of the game and coaching them. Caddying teaches you about discipline and respect. It teaches you how to follow the rules and be honest. These morals and values aren't being taught these days, and I hope to make an impact on kids.

I'm living in St. Augustine, Florida, now, and you can find me on walking the old town streets on a weekend evening and somewhere around a golf course during the day. I enjoy going to the Caddyshack Restaurant, talking with Andy Murray, and getting a bite to eat too and from time to time you will see me at the Hammock Beach Wine and Cheese Shop on A1A in Palm Coast. If you're in town and you see a 6'4" old man in a Stetson hat, say hi!

Alfred "Rabbit" Dyer

Rabbit at 2013 PGA Show

Chi Chi Rodriguez and Rabbit

Chi Chi Rodriguez, John Downing and Rabbit Dyer

Rabbit at World Golf Village

Murray Brothers Caddyshack
World Golf Village
Saint Augustine Florida 2012

Rabbit and John Downing

Rabbit at World Golf Village

Rabbit Dyer and Kary Adams
Murray Brothers Caddyshack

Rabbit finds an old friend,Exie
The World Golf Hall of Fame

Hammock Beach, Florida

The Hammock Beach Wine and Cheese Shoppe
Hammock Beach Florida

Rabbit and fans

Rabbit and Damian

Hammock Beach, Florida

Rabbit and fans
The Hammock Beach Wine and Cheese Shoppe
Hammock Beach Florida 2012

Photos by John Downing

John Downing

John Downing with Dad, Joe Downing 2009

About The Author

Dad was an Ohio State University Alumnus, grew up in Upper Arlington, and went to school with Barbara Nicklaus. I spoke with Barbara recently at the Liberty Mutual Legends of Golf and she had so many memories of them in school. I had always heard stories that Dad introduced her to Jack on a double date and it was hard to believe until I spent the afternoon with her. They had always stayed friends, and when we would see her at tournaments she always invited us to walk with her and follow Jack. When I was thirteen I got a package in the mail for my birthday. I opened it to find a framed autographed picture of Jack Nicklaus. He signed it, "To John, Best of Luck...Jack!"

John Downing

Barbara Nicklaus and John Downing
Liberty Mutual Legends of Golf 2013

My Dad loved to play golf and with his new job in advertising, we were fortunate to be members of Hillcrest Country Club, where my brother, Mark, and I learned to play. I think I got my first set of clubs when I was four years old.

Well, Dad traveled often on business and played in a lot of pro-ams. He took my brother and me to golf tournaments every summer. While he was entertaining clients, Mark and I would walk the courses and follow our favorite golfers, usually Jack Nicklaus, Lee Trevino, Gary Player, Arnold Palmer, Dave Stockton, Raymond Floyd, Tom Weiskopf, and Chi Chi Rodriguez. We would see who could get the most autographs. We even got to walk eighteen holes with Lee Trevino when Dad was partnered up with him at the Colonial one summer.

I was always just as fascinated with the caddies as I was with the pros. I thought it would be such a cool job to walk beside Jack or Gary and help them win. When I couldn't get a pro to sign my program, I would get the caddie's autographs, and at the 1977 US Open in Tulsa, I got Angelo Argea's and a big tall guy named Rabbit. Who would know that he would go on to be one of the most legendary caddies of all time, that I would become his friend thirty-five years later, and that I would write this book.

A year later we moved to Raleigh, North Carolina. We lived behind the first green on the Oaks Course at Northridge Country Club. When I was fifteen the LPGA held the American Defender Classic at Northridge and this is where my caddie dream came true. I was able to caddie for Cindy Chamberlain and, the next year, for Kathy Whitworth. That was 1981, the last year it was played.

So that's a little about me and how I met Rabbit. We have spent a lot of time together this past year, and as I was listening to all of his stories I just knew someone would need to tell them. It's a privilege to be that person and to be his friend.

John Downing

John Downing

John Downing and Rabbit Dyer Christmas 2012

CPSIA information can be obtained at www.ICGtesting.com
Printed in the USA
LVOW01s0641300913

354685LV00009B/19/P

9 781935 795179